A Joke for Every Day of the Year

Sandy Ransford has been hooked on humour ever since her first job in publishing – editing the jokes for a well-known magazine – and she has now written more joke books than she can count. Born in South Yorkshire (which may account for it), she now lives in rural mid-Wales surrounded by sheep, with her husband, a horse, a cat, two pygmy goats and two miniature ponies – all of which keep her laughing.

Peter Allen was a very serious illustrator before he did the drawings for this very funny book. He used to do pictures for scientists' text books full of tiny things you only see down an enormous microscope. He also drew for mathematicians who like their books full of extremely long sums to have a few squiggly pictures here and there. He now spends most of the day laughing, cracking jokes or watching cartoons on the telly.

D1463927

Other Books by Sandy Ransford

Alien Jokes
School Jokes
Football Jokes
The Knock Knock Joke Book
2001: A Joke Odyssey
Spooky Jokes
There's a Fly in My Soup!

A Joke for Every Day of the Year

Sandy Ransford

MACMILLAN CHILDREN'S BOOKS

First published 2002
by Macmillan Children's Books
a division of Macmillan Publishers Limited
20 New Wharf Road London N1 9RR
Basingstoke and Oxford
www.panmacmillan.com

Associated companies throughout the world

ISBN 0 330 48351 X

5 7 9 8 6

A CIP catalogue record for this book is available from the British Library.

Printed by Mackays of Chatham plc, Chatham, Kent.

Contents

JANUARY

Knock, knock.
Who's there?
Snow.
Snow who?
Snow use, I can't remember.

January 1

Angry neighbour: Didn't you hear me hammering on your wall last night?
Smiling neighbour: Oh, that's all right, we had a bit of a party and made quite a lot of noise ourselves.

January 2

Mrs Flivver had just returned from the January sales. 'Were the shops busy?' asked her husband.

'They certainly were,' replied Mrs Flivver. 'One was so crowded two women were trying on the same dress!'

January 3

First sales shopper: Look out! Who do you think you're pushing?

Second sales shopper: I don't know. What's your name?

January 4

Where does Tarzan buy his clothes?
At a January jungle sale.

January 5

What do people sing at a snowman's birthday party?
'Freeze a jolly good fellow.'

January 6

January 6th, the Feast of the Epiphany, is traditionally the time when people take down the Christmas decorations. But one year, little Herbie's dog managed to grab the decorations off the tree and eat them. Do you know what happened to him afterwards? He got tinselitis!

January 7

What do you get if you cross a snowman with a piranha fish?
Frostbite.

January 8

What kind of fish is useful
in icy weather?
A skate.

January 9

Wesley: Did you learn how to ski in Austria?
Lesley: Sort of. But by the time I'd got the hang of standing up I couldn't sit down.

January 10

What happens when you slip and fall down on the ice?
You get thaw.

January 11

Bobbie: How long did it take you to learn to skate?
Robbie: Oh, a few sittings.

January 12

Harold: I'm not going back to that school again.
Mother: Why not?
Harold: It's our maths teacher. On Wednesday she said five and five make ten. Yesterday she said seven and three make ten. And today she said six and four make ten. I'm not going back until she makes up her mind!

January 13

What do you call a building that has a lot of storeys?
A library.

January 14

Man in street: Can you tell me the quickest way to the post office?
Passer-by: Run as fast as you can.

January 15

Which animal with no sense of direction got off a train at the wrong London station and never became famous?
Euston Bear.

January 16

A lady was sitting on a bus next to a little girl who kept sniffing. After a while she said to the child, 'Haven't you got a handkerchief?'

'Oh, yes,' replied the girl, 'but I'm not supposed to lend it to strangers.'

January 17

Why do elephants have wrinkled knees?
Have you ever tried ironing an elephant?

January 18

Tammy: What's the weather like out there?
Sammy: It's so foggy I can't tell.

January 19

Gill: I heard your teacher was dangerously ill last week.
Bill: Yes, but this week he's dangerously better again.

January 20

What's white and goes upwards?
A snowflake with no sense of direction.

January 21

Tommy: Mum! My socks have got holes in them!
Mum: How else would you get your feet in them?

January 22

How do you get 100 Pikachus on a minibus?
Poke-em-on.

January 23

Why couldn't the sailors play
cards?
Because the captain was
standing on the deck.

January 24

The teacher was getting a
bit fed up with little
Freddie, who kept asking
silly questions. 'I can't
answer any more
of your questions
now,' she said firmly.
'Remember, curiosity
killed the cat.'

'Really?' said Freddie. 'What did the cat want to
know?'

January 25

Benny: I had this strange dream last night. I dreamt I was eating some very hard, crunchy sweets.
Jenny: Did they taste nice?
Benny: No. And when I woke up all the buttons on my pyjamas had disappeared!

January 26

Wayne: I just swallowed a bone.
Jayne: Are you choking?
Wayne: No, I'm serious!

January 27

What's a barbecue?
A line of men waiting to get their hair cut.

January 28

Eddie: Why did you throw away your alarm clock?
Teddy: It always went off when I was asleep.

January 29

Why did the lottery millionaire not have a bathroom in his house?
He was filthy rich.

January 30

Andy: Why do they call your brother a miracle worker?
Mandy: Because it's a miracle if they get him to do any work.

January 31

What do you call a woman with two toilets on her head?
Lulu.

FEBRUARY

What's worse than raining cats and dogs?
Hailing taxis

February 1

Jim: Which month has 28 days?
John: They all do!

February 2

What did the baby
hedgehog say
when it backed
into a cactus?
'Is that you,
Mum?'

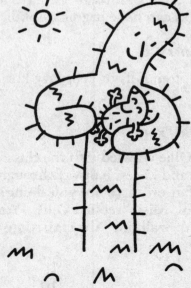

February 3

What do you call a highwayman who has flu?
Sick Turpin.

February 4

Gillie: What a great jacket!
Tilly: Thanks. It's a hunting jacket.
Gillie: It doesn't look like one. Why do you call it that?
Tilly: Because when my sister finds it's gone she'll be hunting for it.

February 5

Suresh: May I share your sledge?
Sheila: Yes, we'll go halves.
Suresh: Thanks, that's great.
Sheila: That's all right. I'll have it going downhill and you can have it going uphill.

February 6

What often falls in February but doesn't get hurt?
Snow.

February 7

Little Ollie crawled into the classroom one day on his hands and knees, halfway through the first lesson.

'What on earth are you doing?' asked the teacher.

'Well, Miss,' replied Ollie. 'Yesterday you told me never to walk into the classroom late again, so I'm not!'

February 8

Herbert: Would you like to borrow my pocket calculator?
Harold: No, thanks, I already know how many pockets I've got.

February 9

Knock, knock.
Who's there?
Lena.
Lena who?
Lena bit closer, I'll tell you a secret.

February 10

Winston: I used to snore so loudly I'd wake myself up.
William: And how did you cure yourself?
Winston: I moved into the next room.

February 11

Paddy: Weren't you learning to tap dance?
Maddie: Yes, but I gave it up.
Paddy: Why?
Maddie: I kept falling into the sink.

February 12

Diner: Waiter! There's a fly in my butter!
Waiter: That's impossible, sir.
Diner: No, it isn't, I just saw it.
Waiter: I'm afraid it is, we only use margarine in this restaurant.

February 13

Susie and Sarah were looking for Valentine cards to send to their boyfriends.

'This one's nice,' said Susie. 'Look, it says, "To the only boy I've ever loved".'

'Yes, that'll do,' replied Sarah. 'I'll take half a dozen.'

February 14

Trixie: I got 20 Valentine cards!
Tilly: I got 30 but I couldn't afford to post them all.

February 15

What's the definition of a teacher?
A person who talks in someone else's sleep.

February 16

Freddie's mum took him to the doctor's because he was covered in spots. 'I think it must be something he's eaten,' said the mother. 'Can you get rid of them for him?'

The doctor examined Freddie. 'Hmm,' he replied. 'I'm afraid I can't make any rash promises.'

February 17

Brian: I'm not myself today.
Ryan: I thought I'd noticed an improvement.

February 18

What's a slug?
A snail with a housing problem.

February 19

What do you get if you cross a mouse with a bottle of washing-up liquid?
Bubble and squeak.

February 20

What do cats rest their heads on at night?
Caterpillars.

February 21

What do cats read at breakfast time?
Mewspapers.

February 22

Knock, knock.
Who's there?
Scott.
Scott who?
Scott nothing to do with you.

February 23

Salesman at door: This gadget will cut your
housework in half, madam.
Woman at door: Sounds great! I'll take two of
them.

February 24

What nut has no shell?
A doughnut.

February 25

What do you call two turnips who fall in love?
Swedehearts.

February 26

The three bears were in the kitchen about to have breakfast. 'Who's been eating my porridge?' asked Father Bear, looking at his empty bowl.

'And who's been eating *my* porridge?' asked Baby Bear, looking at *his* empty bowl.

'Oh, do be quiet, you two,' said Mother Bear. 'I haven't even made the porridge yet.'

February 27

Two magicians were talking about a colleague who had recently retired. 'And what happened to that daughter of his, the one he used to saw in half?' asked one of the other.

'Last I heard she was living in Birmingham and Edinburgh,' replied his friend.

February 28

How do you tell which end of a worm is the head?
Tickle its middle and see which end smiles.

February 29

Why are kangaroos waiting eagerly for 2004?
Because it's a leap year.

MARCH

One spring day a snail started to climb up a cherry tree. A starling turned to its friend and said, 'Look at that silly snail! He's climbing the tree and there aren't any cherries on it!'

The snail overheard the starling. 'You're right,' he replied. 'But there will be by the time I've climbed it.'

March 1

Why is Wales slowly sinking into the sea?
Because it's full of leeks.

March 2

What did the toothpaste say to the toothbrush?
'Give me a squeeze and I'll meet you outside the tube.'

March 3

What did the west wind say to the north wind?
'Let's play draughts.'

March 4

Why don't they eat ice cream in China?
Have you ever tried eating ice cream with chopsticks?

March 5

Anne: What kind of dog is that?
Dan: It's a police dog.

Anne: It doesn't look much like a police dog to me.
Dan: That's because it's a plain-clothes police dog.

March 6

Teacher: What are you drawing, Sammy?
Sammy: It's a picture of a pony in a field eating grass.
Teacher: I can't see any grass. Where is it?
Sammy: The pony ate it.
Teacher: And I can't see the pony either. Where's he?
Sammy: He went back to his stable. He didn't want to stay in a field where there wasn't any grass.

March 7

Dad: I think our Jimmy got his brains from me, don't you?
Mum: He must have, because I've still got mine!

March 8

Customer: This milk tastes very watery.
Waiter: The cow must have been out in the rain.

March 9

Who wrote *Great Eggspectations*?
Charles Chickens.

March 10

Ginny: Will you join me?
Minnie: Why, are you coming apart?

March 11

Teacher: Take your hands out of your pockets when you speak to me.
Billy: I can't. If I do my trousers will fall down.

March 12

Mrs Muddle: I got a shirt for my husband.
Mrs Puddle: I wish I could make a swap like that.

March 13

A man was driving through a remote mountainous area when his car broke down near a monastery. He went and knocked on the door to see if he could phone for help.

The monk who answered the door showed him where the phone was, and then asked him if he'd like to eat with them while he was waiting. The man accepted eagerly, as he was very hungry. They had some delicious fish and chips, which tasted better than any the traveller had eaten before, so he went to the kitchen to congratulate the cook. 'Are you the fish frier?' he asked the brother who was working in there.

'No,' he replied, 'I'm the chip monk.'

March 14

Little Robin was running up and down in the library and making a great deal of noise. The librarian walked up to him and said, 'Shhh! You're making too much noise. The people in here can't read.'

Robin looked around at them. 'Oh dear,' he said. 'They can't be very clever. I could read when I was five.'

March 15

Wes: When did Caesar reign?
Les: I didn't know he rained.
Wes: Of course he did. Didn't they hail him?

March 16

Trev: How did you come to fall in the water?
Kev: I didn't come to fall in the water, I came to fish.

March 17

When does an Irish potato change its nationality? When it becomes a French fry.

March 18

Naval Recruitment Officer: Can you swim?
Would-be Recruit: Why, don't you have any ships?

March 19

What is flat, yellow, and flies round the kitchen at 1,000 km per hour?
An Unidentified Flying Omelette.

March 20

Billy: I went to that art exhibition last week.
Milly: Gauguin?
Billy: No, once was enough.

March 21

Annie: Have you heard the spring song?
Danny: Is that the one that goes, 'Boing, boing'?

March 22

What's grey and yellow, grey and yellow, grey and yellow?
An elephant rolling down a hill with a daffodil in its mouth.

March 23

What did one ear say to the other?
'Between you and me we need a haircut.'

March 24

Teacher: Who knows where Tasmania is? Can you point it out on the globe, Harold?
Harold: There, sir!
Teacher: Well done, Harold. Now, who can tell me who discovered Tasmania?
Henry: Harold, sir.

March 25

Dick: Have you forgotten that you owe me £5?
Mick: Not yet. Give me time and I will.

March 26

Queenie: Our new kitten has a pedigree.
Rene: You mean you have papers for it?
Queenie: Yes, all over the house.

March 27

An old lady went to the post office to collect her pension. As she didn't have a pen, she signed for the money in pencil. The clerk looked at it, then passed it back, saying, 'Would you mind inking it over, Mrs Tiddles?'

The old lady moved to one side for a while, then returned to the counter. 'I've thought it over,' she said, 'and I'd still like my pension, please.'

March 28

What happened to the man who swallowed a torch?
He spat it out again and was de-lighted.

March 29

A man who wanted to buy a parrot went to an
auction of cage birds. He spotted one that looked to
be just what he wanted, and decided to bid for it.
He started the bidding at £5, but another voice
offered £10. So the man offered £15. The voice
topped his bid again, and the two of them went on
like this for some time. Finally, after the man had
offered £50, no more bids were heard. Delighted to
have bought the bird, the man rushed round to
collect it. 'There's just one thing I've forgotten,' he

said to the auctioneer, as he prepared to pay for the parrot, 'does it talk?'

'Of course it does,' replied the auctioneer. 'Who do you think was bidding against you?'

March 30

What's the safest way to use a hammer?
Get someone else to hold the nails.

March 31

What is the most valuable fish in the world?
A goldfish.

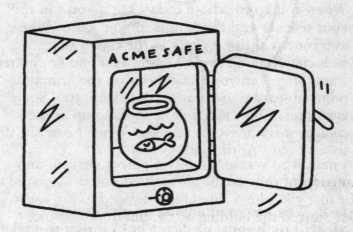

APRIL

*Emma: Are you trying to
make a fool of me?
Gemma: No, I never interfere
with nature.*

April 1

When you go to school today, see if you can fool
your teacher and the people in your class. When
everyone is sitting quietly in the classroom,
suddenly look up at the ceiling as if you've spotted
something. Tap your neighbour on the arm and
point upwards, so he or she looks up, too. Soon
everyone in the class will be looking up at the
ceiling, including your teacher! When he or she does
so, call out, 'April fool!'

April 2

Jack: Why are you jumping up and down?
Mack: I took some medicine but I forgot to shake
the bottle.

April 3

John: What's a football made of?
Don: Pig's hide.

John: Why do they hide?
Don: They don't. I meant the pig's outside.
John: Oh, well, bring him in. Any friend of yours is a friend of mine.

April 4

What did one chimney say to the other?
'If I were you I'd stop smoking.'

April 5

First fortune-teller: What lovely weather we're having.
Second fortune-teller: Yes. It reminds me of the spring of 2005.

April 6

Why is it difficult to talk to your friend in front of a goat?
It always butts in.

April 7

Teacher: Where's your pencil, Graham?
Graham: I haven't got none.
Teacher, sighing: Oh dear. I've told you over and over again not to say that. We say, 'I haven't got any.' Or, 'I do not have a pencil, you do not have a pencil, he or she does not have a pencil.' Do you understand?
Graham: No. Who pinched all our pencils?

April 8

Ken: I can't decide whether to ask Kate or Edith to marry me.
Ben: Well, I guess you can't have your Kate and Edith too.

April 9

Why do birds in the nest always agree?
Because they don't want to fall out.

April 10

Knock, knock.
Who's there?
Doughnut.
Doughnut who?
Doughnut ask me silly questions!

April 11

Little Jenny offered to do the washing-up, but when she put the first plate in the bowl she quickly pulled out her hand, yelling, 'Ouch! That water's scalding! It burnt my hand!'

'Serves you right,' said her brother. 'You should have felt it before you put your hand in it.'

April 12

Ollie: Did you hear the car workers are going on strike?
Molly: What for?

Ollie: Shorter hours.
Molly: Good for them. I've always thought 60 minutes was too long for one hour.

April 13

When is it bad luck to have a black cat cross your path?
When you're a mouse.

April 14

What happens to many children at Easter?
They get over egg-cited.

April 15

What was the little fish given on Easter Sunday?
An oyster egg.

April 16

Tim: Is it raining outside?
Jim: Well, it doesn't usually rain inside!

April 17

Romeo: Will you marry me?
Juliet: No, but I'll always admire your good taste.

April 18

Freddie: You've just written a cheque for £1,000!
Teddy: Yes, it's a birthday present for my girlfriend.
Freddie: Wow! But you forgot to sign it.
Teddy: No, I didn't. I'm sending it anonymously.

April 19

City boy: The farmer where we're staying is a magician.
Country boy: Why do you say that?
City boy: He told me he was going to turn his cows into a field.

April 20

What has eight legs but can't walk?
Four pairs of trousers.

April 21

Why does Lucy like the letter K?
Because it makes Lucy lucky.

April 22

Susie was writing a thank-you letter to her Auntie Jane for the lovely Easter egg she had sent her when she suddenly stopped.

'What's wrong?' asked her mother.

'It was on the tip of my tongue and now it's gone,' replied Susie.

'Well, if you think about it hard enough it'll come back,' said her mother soothingly.

'That won't bring it back,' said Susie sadly. 'I swallowed the stamp!'

April 23

Visiting lecturer: Now, would anyone like to ask any questions?
Cheeky Charlie: Yes, when are you going home?

April 24

What has a bottom at its top?
A leg.

April 25

A shopkeeper who had got into a terrible financial muddle went to see an accountant. After going through the shopkeeper's books, the accountant said, 'This doesn't look too bad, Mr Brown. If you pay my fee of £400, I'll sort this out and do all your worrying for you.'

'Fine,' said Mr Brown. 'It's a deal.' And he prepared to leave the accountant's office.

'Er, where's my £400?' asked the accountant.

'Ah,' replied Mr Brown, 'that's your first worry.'

April 26

John was having driving lessons. His friend Ron asked him if he was taking his test soon.

'Yes,' replied John, 'but my instructor thinks it'll be a close thing.'

'Why's that?' asked Ron.

'Well,' said John, 'I've got four more lessons, and they've only got three more cars.'

April 27

Judge: Have you ever stolen anything before?

Prisoner in the dock: Yes, now and then.

Judge: What have you stolen?

Prisoner: Oh, this and that.

Judge: Take him away and lock him up!

Prisoner: But when will I get out again?

Judge: Oh, sooner or later.

April 28

Mrs Nosy: Can you tell me any more gossip about our new neighbours?

Mrs Waggletongue: No. I've already told you more than I've heard myself.

April 29

Scout leader: Can anyone tell me how to light a fire with two sticks?
Smart alec: Make sure one of them's a match.

April 30

What did one dolphin say to the other as they bumped into each other?
'Did you do that on porpoise?'

MAY

Can February march?
No, but April may.

May 1

John: I used to wear a flower in my buttonhole, but I had to stop.
Don: Why?
John: The pot kept hitting me in the chest.

May 2

Why are garden flowers lazy?
They spend all their lives in beds.

May 3

What kind of flowers does everybody have?
Tulips!

May 4

What do you call a girl who gambles?
Betty.

May 5

Knock, knock.
Who's there?
Cook.
Cook who?
That's the first one I've heard this year!

May 6

Where did the sick gnome go?
To the Elf Centre.

May 7

A man walked into a bar. What did he say?
'Ouch!'

May 8

What do you get if you cross a skunk with a boomerang?
An awful smell you can't get rid of.

May 9

What should you do if the M6 is closed?
Drive up the M3 twice.

May 10

What's green and bounces round the garden?
A spring onion.

May 11

What two words have the most letters?
Post office.

May 12

Sally: Where are you going, Mum?
Mum: I'm taking your brother to the doctor, I don't like the look of him.

Sally: I'll come with you. I don't like the look of him either.

May 13

In which job do you start at the top and work your way down?
Deep-sea diving.

May 14

Teacher: Who wrote *David Copperfield*?
Rude boy: How the Dickens should I know!

May 15

Teacher: What's a Laplander?
William: Someone standing on a crowded bus when it stops suddenly.

May 16

Teacher: Why are you late for school again?
Dopey Dora: I'm afraid I overslept.
Teacher: You mean you sleep at home as well?

May 17

What do kangaroos have that other animals don't have?
Baby kangaroos.

May 18

How does an intruder get into the house?
Intruder window.

May 19

Darren: Hollow!
Sharon: What's hollow?
Darren: An empty greeting.

May 20

How do you make a banana split?
Cut it in half.

May 21

Why do bees have sticky hair?
They use honey combs.

May 22

Knock, knock.
Who's there?
Dishes.
Dishes who?
Dishes your friend, open the door.

May 23

What's a hen's favourite TV programme?
The feather forecast.

May 24

How do you use an Egyptian doorbell?
Toot-and-come-in.

May 25

'Doctor, doctor, I think I'm getting smaller.'
'You'll just have to be a little patient.'

May 26

Knock, knock.
Who's there?
Canoe.
Canoe who?
Canoe come out and play with me?

May 27

What did the big flower say to the little flower?
'How are you, bud?'

May 28

Mum: Did you enjoy the school trip to London?
Jimmy: Oh, yes, but we've got to go back again
tomorrow.
Mum: Why's that?
Jimmy: To see if we can find the kids that got left
behind.

May 29

Louise: You remind me of the sea.
Larry: Why? Because I'm wild, untamed and
romantic?
Louise: No, because you make me sick.

May 30

Wayne: Have you heard the new band Instant Potato?
Jayne: No.
Wayne: They had a Smash Hit!

May 31

Aunty Clara: Where's your sister, Freddie?
Freddie: She's still in the living room playing our piano duet. I finished first.

JUNE

Mandy: Light from the sun
travels at 186,000 miles an
hour. Isn't that amazing?
Andy: Not really. It's downhill
all the way.

June 1

Terry: How much am I worth to you, Mum?
Mum: You're worth a million pounds, Terry.
Terry: In that case, would you lend me ten of them?

June 2

Teacher: Where are English kings and queens crowned?
Bertie: On the head.

June 3

Three pieces of string decided they'd like a cup of tea, so they went into a café. The first went up to the counter to order, but the waitress said, 'We don't serve pieces of string in here, just people.'

So the second piece of string tried to order, but the waitress refused to serve him also.

The third piece of string thought for a moment, tied himself into a knot, and unravelled some of its ends. He then approached the counter. 'Are you another piece of string?' asked the waitress suspiciously.

'No,' he replied, 'I'm a frayed knot.'

June 4

What's a frog's favourite sweet?
A lollihop.

June 5

What bird works in a kitchen?
A cook-coo.

June 6

What kind of dog goes into a corner when a bell rings?
A boxer.

June 7

A theatre manager was interviewing an entertainer.
'And did you say you could play the piano?' he
asked.

'Oh, yes,' replied the entertainer. 'I've played for
more than 20 years, on and off.'

'Slippery stool?' asked the manager.

June 8

Which is the left side of a fruit pie?
The side that isn't eaten.

June 9

Johnny: A man called to see you while you were
out.
Dad: Did he have a bill?
Johnny: No, just an ordinary nose like anyone else.

June 10

What do you call a camel with three humps?
Humphrey.

June 11

Boy in bank: Who dropped a roll of notes with a rubber band round them?
Several bank customers: I did!
Boy in bank: Well, here's the rubber band.

June 12

Mrs Tinkle: Go and ask our neighbour if you can borrow his bagpipes.
Mr Tinkle: But I can't play them!
Mrs Tinkle: No, but neither can he while you've got them.

June 13

Teacher: Who knows what an atom is?
Dilly: Wasn't he the man who lived with Eve?

June 14

What do you get if you cross an ant colony with a flowerbed?
Ants in your plants.

June 15

Peter: How do you spell 'enrietta?
Paul: You mean Henrietta?
Peter: No, I've written the H already.

June 16

Bobbie: I got 100 per cent at school today.
Mum: Well done! What did you get 100 per cent in?

Bobbie: Well, actually it was in two things. I got 50 per cent in geography and 50 per cent in history.

June 17

Harry: My girlfriend's a twin.
Larry: How do you tell them apart?
Harry: Her brother's got a beard.

June 18

Mother: It's time for your violin lesson.
Sammy: Oh, fiddle!

June 19

Who invented the four-day week?
Robinson Crusoe – he had all his work done by Friday.

June 20

What's the best thing for water on the knee?
Drainpipe trousers.

June 21

What has eight legs, two arms, two wings and three heads?
A man on a horse carrying a chicken.

June 22

Terry: They say eating too many sweets affects the brain.
Jerry: You're crazy!

June 23

What always succeeds?
A bird with no teeth.

June 24

Did you hear about the man who stayed up all night on Midsummer's Day to see what happened to the sun when it went down? It finally dawned on him.

June 25

How can you tell the age of a telephone?
By counting its rings.

June 26

A visitor to Egypt was fascinated by the exhibits in the local museum. 'Whose skull is that?' she asked the guide, pointing at the bones in a showcase.

'That is the skull of the great queen Cleopatra,' explained the guide.

'And whose is the small skull beside it?' persisted the tourist.

'That is the skull of the great queen Cleopatra when she was a little girl,' replied the guide proudly.

June 27

Three old boys from a remote village were travelling on a train to London. They'd never been to London before, and they'd never been on a train before, either. Just as they were boarding the train, the son of one of them, who had brought them to the station, handed his father a bunch of bananas to eat on the journey. When they were settled in their seats, the old man handed round the bananas, and began to peel his and eat it. It was the first time he'd ever tasted the fruit.

Just as he bit into it, the train entered a tunnel. 'Hey, Bill,' he called to one of his pals, 'have you tried your banana yet?'

'Not yet,' replied Bill.

'Well, don't,' said the first man. 'I took one bite of mine and went blind.'

June 28

Gardener: This is a dogwood tree.
Visitor: How can you tell?
Gardener: By its bark.

June 29

Why is tennis such a noisy game?
Because every player raises a racket.

June 30

Jane: Do you think I'm vain?
Wayne: No. Why do you ask?
Jane: Because girls as beautiful as me usually are.

JULY

*Dad: How did you get that big red lump
on your nose?*
Dave: I got it sniffing a brose.
Dad: A brose? There's no 'b' in rose.
Dave: There was in this one!

July 1

Knock, knock.
Who's there?
Stepfather.
Stepfather who?
One stepfather and I'll be in.

July 2

Why did the boy
keep his guitar in
the fridge?
Because he liked
to play it cool.

July 3

Did you hear about the car with the wooden wheels and the wooden engine?
It wooden go.

July 4

What's the best way to raise strawberries?
With a spoon.

July 5

Passer-by: What's the matter, little boy?
Little boy, sobbing: I swapped my pet mouse for a bottle of pop because I was thirsty.
Passer-by: And now you wish you hadn't?
Little boy: Yes.
Passer-by: Because you realize you loved your little mouse and you miss him?
Little boy: No, because I'm thirsty again.

July 6

Mrs Smith: Who was that on the phone?
Mr Brown: Just someone who said it was long distance from the United States, but I told him I knew that and hung up.

July 7

First vampire: How are things with you?
Second vampire: Not so good.
First vampire: Why, what's the matter?
Second vampire: I've just had a letter from the

blood bank – I'm
overdrawn 100 litres.

July 8

A man knocked on the door of a house and asked
the lady who answered if she could spare some
food. She studied his face. 'Didn't I give you a meat
pie last week?' she asked.

'Yes,' replied the man, 'but I've recovered now.'

July 9

A farmer spotted two boys in one of his fields. 'Oi,'
he yelled, 'don't you know you're trespassing?
Didn't you read the notice?'

'Yes,' answered one boy, 'but it said Private so
we didn't like to read any more.'

July 10

What's green and hairy and wears sunglasses?
A gooseberry on holiday.

July 11

What did one rose bush say to the other?
'Take me to your weeder.'

July 12

Baby cabbage: Where did I come from?
Mother cabbage: The stalk brought you.

July 13

Which side of a hedgehog is the most prickly?
The outside.

July 14

Jim: Did you hear about the man who tried to swim the Channel last week?
Slim: No, did he make it?
Jim: No. Two kilometres from the French coast he felt so tired he turned back.

July 15

Maeve: It's St Swithin's Day, and it's raining cats and dogs!
Dave: I know, I just stepped in a poodle.

July 16

Vicar: I hear you were out playing cricket yesterday instead of coming to church.
Little boy: No, I wasn't, honestly – and what's more I've got the fish to prove it.

July 17

Billy came home from school complaining of stomach-ache. 'That's because your stomach's empty,' said his mum. 'You'll feel much better when you've got something inside it.'

A little later his father came home complaining of a headache. 'That's because your head's empty,' explained Billy, soothingly. 'You'll feel a lot better when you've got something inside it.'

July 18

What can travel round the world while remaining in the same corner?
A postage stamp.

July 19

Did you hear about the two men who ran in the fathers' race at the school sports day?
One ran in short bursts, the other in burst shorts.

July 20

First neighbour: Are you painting your living room this afternoon?
Second neighbour: Yes.
First neighbour: In that case, may I borrow your tennis racket? You won't be needing it!

July 21

Two little boys were having their first cricket lesson.
'How do you hold the bat?' asked one.
    'By the wings, of course,' replied his friend.

July 22

Why do bees hum?
Because they can't
remember the words.

humm
m
m
m
m

July 23

What has four legs
but only one foot?
A bed.

July 24

Father: Your
school report isn't
as good as it was
last term. Why's that?
Andy: Oh, that's the teacher's
fault.
Father: But I thought you had the same teacher as
last term?
Andy: We do. But she moved the school swot to the
front row – and he used to sit next to me!

July 25

Marty: I'm going to save you some money, Mum.
Mum: Wonderful! How will you do that?

Marty: Well, remember how you told me you'd give me £20 if I passed my exams?
Mum: Yes.
Marty: Er, you don't have to pay me.

July 26

Have you heard the story about the peacock?
It's a beautiful tail.

July 27

Why is M every schoolkid's favourite letter?
Because it's the end of TERM.

July 28

Jen: How did you manage to break your ankle?
Ken: You see those steps by the back door?
Jen: Yes.
Ken: I didn't.

July 29

Knock, knock.
Who's there?
Aniseed.
Aniseed who?
Aniseed you eating
all those
strawberries!

July 30

A party of schoolboys were going on a trip to
France, and when they got on the ferry one of the
teachers accompanying them got them up on deck
to run through the safety drill.

'What would you do if a child falls overboard?'
she asked.

'Shout, "Boy overboard!" ' answered young
Lester.

'Good,' said the teacher. 'And what would you
do if a teacher falls overboard?'

'Er, which one, Miss?' replied the cheeky child.

July 31

Davey: How much pocket money can I have in the
holidays?
Father: Seventy-five pence a week.
Davey: Seventy-five pence a week! That's an insult!
Father: OK, I'll give it to you monthly so you won't
feel insulted so often.

AUGUST

Nellie: Why are you looking over the top of your sunglasses instead of through them?
Kelly: I don't want to wear them out.

August 1

Dave: Look at all the water in that lake!
Maeve: Yes, and that's only the top of it.

August 2

Jenny: What did the high tide say to the low tide?
Kenny: 'Lo, tide.
Jenny: And what did the low tide say to the high tide?
Kenny: Hi, tide.
Jenny: Then what did they say?
Kenny: Nothing, they just waved.

August 3

Mary: Monty's parents are sending him to his penfriend's for the summer.
Cary: Does he need a holiday?
Mary: No, but his parents do.

August 4

Jen: I love sunbathing, don't you?
Ken: Oh, yes. I could sit in the sun all day and all night.

August 5

First camper: How's your holiday home?
Second camper: OK, but it's a bit small.
First camper: So's ours. The kitchen's so tiny we have to use condensed milk.

August 6

A man went swimming in the sea and when he came out he discovered that all his clothes had been stolen. What did he go home in?
The dark!

August 7

What did the koala take on holiday?
Just the bear essentials.

August 8

Ed: I feel like a cup of tea.
Ted: You look like one too – wet, weak and sloppy.

August 9

Jim: My auntie's gone to the West Indies for her holidays.
Tim: Jamaica?
Jim: No, she went of her own free will.

August 10

Mrs Flather: So you're not going to the south of France for your holidays?
Mrs Flither: No, that was last year. This year we're not going to Spain.

August 11

Mr and Mrs Round were waiting at the airport when Mrs Round suddenly said, 'I wish I'd brought the TV with us.'

'What on earth makes you say that?' asked Mr Round.

'I left the plane tickets on it.'

August 12

Connie: Did you enjoy your week in Greece?
Ronnie: Yes, but it was so hot we had to take turns sitting in each other's shadows.

August 13

Johnny: How was your holiday hotel?
Donny: I got a nice room with a bath.
Johnny: That sounds all right.
Donny: Yes, the problem was they were in different buildings.

August 14

What's the best thing to put in an ice cream soda?
A straw!

August 15

Knock, knock.
Who's there?
Felix.
Felix who?
Felix my ice cream again I'll bop him one.

August 16

Why doesn't the sea fall over the horizon?
It's tied.

August 17

What did one rock pool say to the other when the
tide went out?
'Show us your mussels.'

August 18

What happened to the little boy who ran away with
the circus?
The police made him bring it back.

August 19

Plane passenger: Does this plane fly faster than
sound?
Flight attendant: No, sir.
Plane passenger: That's good, because I want to
talk to my friend.

August 20

Mr and Mrs Muddle and their children were staying
at a guest house at the seaside. One day they'd been
on a trip and on the way home their car broke down,
making them very late getting back. When they
arrived at the guest house, the door was locked and
all the windows were dark. Mr Muddle knocked on
the door several times, then banged on a window and
called out loudly. Eventually a window opened and a
head looked out. 'What do you want?' it snarled.

'We're the Muddles, we're staying here,' replied
Mr Muddle.

'Then stay there, then!' shouted the landlady,
slamming the window shut.

August 21

Don: Was it hot when you were in Greece?
Ron: I'll say! It was so hot the cows gave evaporated milk!

August 22

Traffic warden: Why did you park your car here?
Motorist: Because the sign says 'Fine for parking'.

August 23

Harold: My uncle owns a newspaper.
Horace: So what? A newspaper only costs 30p!

August 24

Pattie: My Canadian grandfather once got up in the night and shot a bear in his pyjamas.
Mattie: What was a bear doing in his pyjamas?

August 25

Tilly: Look at that flock of cows.
Milly: Not flock, herd.
Tilly: Herd what?
Milly: Herd of cows.
Tilly: Of course I've heard of cows.

August 26

Dave: Why did you come home early from your holiday?
Maeve: Well, we were staying on a farm. The first day a cow died and we had beef for dinner. The second day a pig died and we had pork for dinner. The third day the farmer died, so we left.

August 27

Where do ghosts go on bank holidays?
Lake Erie.

August 28

First fisherman: I tell you, it was that long. I never saw a fish like that!
Second fisherman: I believe you.

August 29

Mrs Mumble: Our holiday home didn't have a flaw.
Mrs Tumble: What did you walk on, then?

August 30

Holly: Do you think mosquitoes have brains?
Molly: Well, they certainly seem to be able to work out where we're having a picnic.

August 31

Nick: I can't decide whether to go to a palmist or a mind-reader.
Mick: If I were you I'd go to a palmist. At least you know you've got a palm.

SEPTEMBER

*Some boy scouts were crossing a field
full of cows when their leader realized
that little Jimmy had got left behind. He
waited for him to catch up, and then
asked what the problem had been.*

*'Well,' said little Jimmy, 'my beret
blew off and I had to try on six before I
found it.'*

September 1

Gamekeeper: Oi! There's no fishing allowed in this
river!
Little boy: I'm not fishing, I'm teaching my pet
maggot to swim.

September 2

What's the address for the Morse Code web site?
Dot, dot, dot, dash, dash, dash, dot. com.

September 3

Mum: Have you been fighting again, Lionel? You've lost your front teeth!
Lionel: No, I haven't, they're in my pocket.

September 4

'Waiter! My lobster's only got one claw!'
'It must have been in a fight, sir.'
'Then bring me the winner.'

September 5

Mum: And how did you enjoy your first day at school, Johnny?
Johnny: First day? You mean I have to go back there again?

September 6

Kenton: Are you coming out to play?
Fenton: No, I'm helping Mum do my homework.

September 7

Dad: I'll give you 50p to clean my car this week, and if you do it next week I'll raise it to 75p.
Son: Great! I'll start next week.

September 8

'Doctor, my wooden leg is giving me a lot of pain.'
'Why's that?'
'My wife keeps hitting me over the head with it.'

September 9

How do you start a teddy bear race?
'Ready, teddy, go!'

September 10

When is a teacher like a bird of prey?
When she watches you like a hawk.

September 11

Who invented the sword dance?
Someone who wanted to dance and cut his toenails
at the same time.

September 12

Did you hear about the man who went into a pet shop and asked if they had any kittens going cheap? The assistant replied that only the canaries went cheep.

September 13

Mum: Why is your sister crying?
Mike: Because I said she was stupid.
Mum: That was very unkind of you. Tell her you're sorry.
Mike: I'm sorry you're stupid, sis.

September 14

Two friends were taking their first trip abroad. It was also the first time either of them had flown in a plane. 'If this plane turns upside down, will we fall out?' asked the first.

71

'Of course not,' replied the second. 'I'll always be friends with you.'

September 15

What do you get if you dial
021657834298675473890213?
An aching finger.

September 16

Who wrote *Wonderful Holidays in the West Country*?
Gloria Stevvon.

September 17

What do you get if you sit underneath a cow?
A pat on the head.

September 18

What do you call a man with a paper bag on his head?
Russell.

September 19

Mr Dum: I hear you went to Venice for your holidays. How did you enjoy it?
Mr Dim: Oh, we only stayed a couple of days. The whole place was flooded.

September 20

Mrs Tripp: I hear your son's in the school football team.
Mrs Trapp: That's right.
Mrs Tripp: What position does he play?
Mrs Trapp: I'm not sure, but I think he's one of the drawbacks.

September 21

What did one spider say to the other? 'Welcome to my web-site.'

September 22

What kind of tree can you find in the house?
A pantry.

September 23

Hattie: Mum, what was the name of the station the train just stopped at?
Mum: I didn't notice. I was reading. Why do you ask?
Hattie: I thought you'd like to know where my little brother got off.

September 24

Ken: What can I give my sister for her birthday?
Keith: I don't know. What did you give her last year?
Ken: Chickenpox.

September 25

Sally: I've changed my mind.
Wally: I thought there'd been an improvement.

September 26

They say that dogs can talk, but it's not true. If any dog tells you he can talk, he's lying!

September 27

What's the difference between school stew and cat food?
The stew's served on a plate, the cat food in a bowl.

September 28

Tim: Larry's cooking is getting better.
Jim: You mean you can actually eat it?
Tim: No, but the smoke is grey instead of black.

September 29

'Waiter, waiter! Why have you got your thumb on my sandwich?'
'To stop it falling on the floor again, sir.'

September 30

Jen: Did you miss me when I was away?
Ken: Oh, have you been away?

OCTOBER

Gally: Did you hear about the daft man who hurt himself raking up leaves?
Wally: No, how did he do that?
Gally: He fell out of the tree.

October 1

Knock, knock.
Who's there?
Weasel.
Weasel who?
Weasel while you work.

October 2

Andy: I hear your new boyfriend
works in the fish shop.
Mandy: Yes, how did you know?
Andy: He has a certain air about him.

October 3

What's the longest piece of furniture in the world?
A multiplication table.

October 4

Darren, at cinema: Can you see all right?

76

Sharon: Yes, thank you.
Darren: That large man in front isn't blocking your view?
Sharon: No.
Darren: And your seat is comfortable?
Sharon: Oh, yes.
Darren: In that case, would you mind changing places?

October 5

What happened to the cat who ate a ball of wool?
She had mittens.

October 6

Matt: Yes, you can stay the night, but I'm afraid you'll have to make your own bed.
Wat: Oh, that's OK.

Matt: Sure? Well, here's a saw, a hammer and some nails. The wood's in the workshop.

October 7

What's the difference between a buffalo and a bison?
You can't wash your hands in a buffalo.

October 8

Mother: I'd like to meet the boy that gave you that black eye!
Tom: No one gave it to me, Mum, I had to fight for it.

October 9

Teacher: Can you tell me three collective nouns?
Milly: The wastepaper basket, the dustbin and the vacuum cleaner.

October 10

Why did the lady order alphabet soup?
She liked to read while she was eating.

October 11

Teacher: Samantha, if I gave you two rabbits today and three more tomorrow and four more the next day, how many would you have?
Samantha: Ten, Miss.
Teacher: Ten?
Samantha: Yes, I've got one already.

October 12

Two astronauts went up into space. One had to go outside their spacecraft to carry out some repairs, while the other stayed inside. When the outside one wanted to re-enter the craft, he found the door was locked. So he knocked on it, loudly. 'Who's there?' came a voice from inside.

October 13

What did the baby mouse say
when he saw a bat for
the first time?
'Hey, I've just seen
an angel!'

October 14

What's the difference between ammonia and pneumonia?
One comes in bottles, the other comes in chests.

October 15

What do you get if you cross a sheepdog and a
bunch of tulips?
Collie-flowers.

October 16

Boss: Aren't you the same boy who applied for this
job last year?
Boy: Yes, sir.
Boss: Didn't I tell you I needed someone older?
Boy: Yes, sir. That's why I've come back now.

October 17

Mum: Are you writing to your grandma, as I asked
you to?
Jerry: Yes, Mum.

Mum: Good. Why is your writing so large?
Jerry: Well, Grandma's deaf so I'm writing very loud.

October 18

Peter: Is your dog a good watch-dog?
Anita: I guess so. Last week he watched someone burgling our house.

October 19

'Who are you?'
'I'm a piano tuner.'
'But I didn't ask you to call.'
'No, but your neighbour did.'

October 20

First lad: How many fish have you caught today?
Second lad: When I catch another I'll have one.

October 21

Traveller: Where is this train going to?
Porter: This train goes to Edinburgh in ten minutes, sir.

Traveller: Really? Last time I went to Edinburgh it took six hours.

October 22

What kind of animal has wooden legs?
A timber wolf.

October 23

Mrs Smart: Do you like our new swimming pool?
Mrs Smite: Yes, it's beautiful. But why doesn't it have any water in it?
Mrs Smart: We can't swim.

October 24

What can you have in your pocket when it's empty?
A hole!

October 25

Eric: How old were you on your last birthday?
Derek: Seven.
Eric: So you'll be eight on your next birthday?
Derek: No, I'll be nine.
Eric: How come?
Derek: I'm eight today.

October 26

Why did the schoolboy have to get a potato clock?
So he could be at school by nine o'clock.

October 27

Len: I heard a new joke yesterday. Did I tell it to you?
Ken: Is it funny?
Len: Yes.
Ken: Then you didn't.

October 28

Jimmy: That's a pretty loud tie, isn't it?
Timmy: Yes, but I've got a muffler to go with it.

October 29

Where did Mozart live?
In A flat.

October 30

How do you make a bandstand?
Take away their chairs.

October 31

Bill: Would you like to come to our Hallowe'en party?

Jill: Yes, please. Where do you live?

Bill: At 68 Greystones Road. Just push the bell with your elbow.

Jill: Why with my elbow?

Bill: You're not coming empty-handed, are you?

NOVEMBER

Why did Humpty Dumpty have a great fall?
He wanted to make up for his bad summer.

November 1

Mike: I don't know whether to be a poet or a composer.
Spike: Oh, I think you should be a poet.
Mike: Have you read any of my poetry?
Spike: No, but I've heard some of your music.

November 2

Father: I don't know what's happened to my shaving brush. The bristles seem to have shrunk and they're full of little bits.
Son: That's funny, it was fine yesterday when I cleaned out the mouse cage with it.

November 3

A group of tourists was visiting an ancient battleground. Their guide pointed, 'Do you see that rock? That's where King Richard fell.'

'I'm not surprised,' said one of the tourists, 'I almost tripped over it myself.'

November 4

Mr Dimwit went to buy a new washbasin. 'Would you like a plug for it?' asked the salesman.

'A plug?' asked Mr Dimwit. 'I didn't know they made electric basins nowadays.'

November 5

Knock, knock.
Who's there?
Penny.
Penny who?
Penny for the guy.

November 6

Mother: Eat your liver, Charlie, it's full of iron.
Charlie: I expect that's why it's so tough.

November 7

Nigel: I learned to dance in one lesson.
Nina: I thought as much.

November 8

Why do mice squeak?
Because nobody oils them.

November 9

What do you get if you cross a deer with a sheep?
A woolly hat and a peg to hang it on.

November 10

Visitor: Your dog's very friendly. He keeps coming up to me and wagging his tail.
Little Johnny: That's probably because you're eating your pudding out of his bowl.

November 11

Julie: Do you like my dress? It's over 50 years old.
Gilly: Really? Did you make it yourself?

November 12

What do you find up a gum tree?
A stick insect.

November 13

Errol: Are you superstitious?
Beryl: No.
Errol: Then will you lend me £13?

November 14

Why was the bride unlucky?
Because she didn't marry the best man.

November 15

How do you hire a car?
Stand it on four bricks.

November 16

A man took a terrier back to the breeder he bought it from. 'You said this dog would be good for rats,' he complained. 'I've had him three months and he hasn't caught a single one.'

'Well,' replied the breeder. 'That's good for rats, isn't it?'

November 17

Doctor: What did you dream about last night?
Darren: Football.
Doctor: And what did you dream about the night before?
Darren: Football.
Doctor: Don't you ever dream about girls?
Darren: What, and miss my chance at goal?

November 18

What do you call a carousel with no brakes?
A merry-go-round-round-round-round-round-round-round.

November 19

How do you get to be a litter collector?
Oh, you just pick it up as you go along.

November 20

Perry: Why do you say Herbert must have a sixth sense?
Jerry: Well, he shows no signs of having the other five.

November 21

The condemned man was asked if he had any last request. 'Yes,' he replied, 'I'd like permission to sing a song.'

'Permission granted,' said his guard.

So the man began to sing, 'There were nine million, nine hundred and ninety-nine thousand, nine hundred and ninety-nine green bottles hanging on a wall . . .'

November 22

Dennis: Is it true that an apple a day keeps the doctor away?
Dad: I believe so.
Dennis: Then give me an apple quickly, I just kicked my football through the doctor's window!

November 23

Sign on a butcher's shop: Pleased to meet you. Meat to please you.

November 24

What's the difference between a burglar and a church bell?
One steals from the people, the other peals from the steeple.

November 25

A marathon runner ran for an hour but only moved two feet. How come?
He only had two feet!

November 26

Romeo: Darling, will you really put up with my ugly face for the rest of your life?
Juliet: Of course, dear. You'll be out at work all day, won't you?

November 27

'Doctor, doctor, I was playing my mouth-organ and I swallowed it!'

'Look on the bright side, you could have been playing a piano.'

November 28

Did you hear about the woman who went on a high-oil diet?
She didn't lose much weight but she stopped squeaking.

November 29

Mr Fang: This meat is awful, it's so tough.
Mrs Fang: The butcher said it was tender spring lamb.
Mr Fang: That explains it. I must have eaten one of the springs.

November 30

How do baby hens dance?
Chick to chick.

DECEMBER

Three men were stuck in a snowdrift,
but only two got their hair wet. Why?
The third man was bald!

December 1

Jen: You have the face of a saint.
Ken: Really? Which one?
Jen: St Bernard!

December 2

Why can't a bicycle stand up?
Because it's two-tyred.

December 3

Leo: My granny's gone to Indonesia.
Cleo: Jakarta?
Leo: No, she flew there.

December 4

Insurance salesman: This is a very good policy, sir.
We pay £1,000 for broken arms or legs.
Mr Woollybrain: Amazing! What do you do with
them all?

December 5

Bill and Ben were boasting to each other about how important their fathers were.

'*My* father went to see Einstein yesterday,' said Bill.

'But Einstein's dead,' retorted Ben.

'That would explain it,' said Bill. 'Dad said he was very quiet.'

December 6

What did the beaver say to the tree?
'It's been good gnawing you.'

December 7

Milly: Lend me twenty pence, I want to phone a friend.

Tilly: Here's forty pence, phone all your friends.

December 8

Why is a dumbo like blotting paper?
He soaks everything up but gets it all backwards.

December 9

How can you tell the time with a candle?
Listen to the candle's-tick.

December 10

Mother: What would you like for Christmas,
Maureen?
Maureen: I've got my eye on that blue bike in the
shop in the High Street.
Mother: Well, you'd better keep your eye on it
because at the price they're charging you'll never get
your bottom on it!

December 11

First prisoner: Why are you in here?
Second prisoner: I got arrested for doing my
Christmas shopping early.
First prisoner: They can't arrest you for that!
Second prisoner: They can – they caught me in the
jeweller's at two in the morning!

December 12

A woman was looking round a department store when an assistant approached her and asked if she could help. 'Well,' admitted the woman, 'I'm looking for something cheap and vulgar for my mother-in-law.'

'I've got just the thing,' replied the shop assistant, 'my father-in-law!'

December 13

Sammy: Mum, are we having Auntie Ada for Christmas dinner this year?
Mum: No, dear, I thought we'd have a turkey as usual.

December 14

Hamish: Have you ever seen a man-eating fish?
Dougal: Aye.
Hamish: Where?
Dougal: In McTavish's seafood restaurant.

December 15

When is a turkey 20 metres tall?
When he's walking on stilts.

December 16

What part of a fish weighs the most?
Its scales.

December 17

Bert: I can lift an elephant with one hand.
Gert: I don't believe you!
Bert: Get me an elephant with one hand and I'll
show you.

December 18

Doctor: You must take four teaspoons of this
medicine three times a day.
Patient: But we've only got three teaspoons!

December 19

Knock, knock.
Who's there?
Cereal.
Cereal who?
Cereal pleasure to meet you.

December 20

What kind of exams did Santa take?
Ho-ho-ho-levels.

December 21

Gwyn: Are you going to Jerry's party?
Gwen: No. The invitation says 'from four to eight'
and I'm nine.

December 22

What are the best things to put in a Christmas cake?
Your teeth!

December 23

Bella: I wanted to buy my Auntie Jemima handkerchiefs for Christmas but I changed my mind.
Ella: Why?
Bella: I couldn't remember how big her nose was.

December 24

Overheard one Christmas Eve: 'I don't care who you are, you great bearded slob, get those reindeer off my roof instantly!'

December 25

What did one Christmas cracker say to the other?
'My pop's bigger than your pop.'

December 26

What is Santa's wife called?
Mary Christmas.

December 27

Knock, knock.
Who's there?
Godfrey.
Godfrey who?
Godfrey tickets for the pantomime – you coming?

December 28

What did the deaf fisherman get for Christmas?
A herring aid.

December 29

What do you call a reindeer with one eye?
No idea.

December 30

Don: I like kissing girls under the mistletoe.
Ron: I prefer kissing them under the nose.

December 31

Sharon and Darren were attending their first New
Year's Eve party, and had been told they must be
home no more than an hour after midnight. They
kept an eye on the time using Sharon's watch, and
saw the new year in with their friends. After a

while, Darren asked, 'How much after midnight is it now?'

'I don't know,' replied Sharon. 'My watch only goes up to twelve.'

Happy new year!

2001

A JOKE ODYSSEY

The Millennium Joke Book

Sandy Ransford

2001 side-splittingly funny jokes for the

millennium ...

Why did the lobster blush?
Because the seaweed.

What do cannibals do at a wedding?
Toast the bride and groom.

**What can a whole apple do that half an
apple can't do?**
Look round.

**Why was the mushroom invited to
lots of parties?**
He was a fungi to be with.

Why is a football stadium cool?
Because there's a fan in every seat.

What do you call a vicar on a motorbike?
Rev.

What better way to celebrate the millennium than
with this hilarious collection of jokes guarateed to
make you giggle?

Spooky Jokes, Puzzles and Poems

Sandy Ransford and David Orme

Scare yourself silly with a spine-tingling,
spooktacular collection of jokes, puzzles
and petrifying poems.

What do vampires take before going to bed?
A bloodbath.

How does a werewolf sign a letter?
'Best vicious.'

PLUS
Which witch is which?
Decipher the ghoulish message

A SELECTED LIST OF TITLES AVAILABLE FROM MACMILLAN CHILDREN'S BOOKS

SANDY RANSFORD
2001: A JOKE ODYSSEY
The Millennium Joke Book   0 330 34988 0   £3.99
HOLIDAY JOKES   0 330 39771 0   £3.99
SANDY RANSFORD AND DAVID ORME
SPOOKY JOKES, PUZZLES
   AND POEMS   0 330 41340 6   £4.99
ROWLAND MORGAN
ABSOLUTELY MENTAL 2   0 330 48173 8   £2.99

All Pan Macmillan titles can be ordered from our website,
www.panmacmillan.com, or from your local bookshop
and are also available by post from:

Bookpost, PO Box 29, Douglas, Isle of Man IM99 1BQ
Credit cards accepted. For details:
Telephone: 01624 836000
Fax: 01624 670923
E-mail: bookshop@enterprise.net
www.bookpost.co.uk

Free postage and packing in the United Kingdom

Prices shown above were correct at the time of going to press.
However, Macmillan Publishers reserves the right to show
new retail prices on covers which may differ from those
previously advertised in the text or elsewhere.